LIKE WIND INTO AIR

LIKE WIND INTO AIR

Joanie McLean

REDHAWK
PUBLICATIONS

Redhawk Publications
The Catawba Valley Community College Press
2550 US Hwy 70 SE
Hickory NC 28602

ISBN: 978-1-959346-28-9

Library of Congress Number: 2023948416

Printed in the United States of America

Layout by Melanie Johnson Zimmermann

redhawkpublications.com

Cover image: "Yellow Finger Cloud" by Anne Crowley, Anne
Crowley Fine Art https://annebcrowley.com/home.html

Dedication

For Gail
sister, mentor, muse

Table of Contents

III. Each to Each

Like Wind Into Air

The mind apprehends its own emptiness,
fuses with its own emptiness
like water poured into water.

—His Holiness the Dalai Lama

I. The Before Times

...always, unfailing, the meadow lark's call...

Coyote Comes Across the Field

Unmistakable
lupine loping
how do you cover
so much ground
with such nonchalance
steadily coming nearer
so sure of yourself
this crisp fall evening
winding across
the open field
flaunting
self-possession
nearer now

You circle
the persimmon tree
make an uncanny
leap to snatch
a ripe pink fruit
without missing
a saunter's beat
you keep coming
nearer

Taking no trouble
with caution
nary a glance
toward the deck
where I stand
your coat is
silky russet
in the falling light
your eyes
kohl-lined
your grin
the emblem
of your sovereignty
this farm is yours

Hurricane Watch

I hear Sharon at the barn
testing generators
just to be sure.
We've been up to the store
waited in line
to top-off fuel cans,
filled the water buckets
(two or three flushes each)
and the jugs for drinking and coffee.
We've collapsed the deck chairs
and latched the porch door.

At the edge of the field
humming birds work
the ironweed and joe-pye.
The horses move
at leisurely pace
from one sweet patch
to the next
flapping their tails
shivering their withers
to shake off flies.
The cicadas buzz and fizz.
Business as usual
in the field today.

And tonight when the wind rises
and the rains come sideways
shelter will be found
in the woods or hedge rows
or deep down in dense clumps
of broom sedge.
The horses will eschew the barn
stand shoulder to shoulder
at the top of the hill
heads lowered
tails into the storm.

Gently

On the way to town
his thin-lipped smile
appears
in my rear-view mirror
forked tongue flicking
he ducks from view
then the thrill
of cool silk flexing
sliding across
my bare legs

I gently press
the brake pedal
pull off the road
swing wide the car door
a bolt of black lightening
flashes into the grass
and the cuckoo clacks
from the tupelo gum.

Meadow Lark

As time remains free of all that it frames
May your mind stay clear of all that it names.
—John O'Donohue

There is something that happens
every midsummer morning
always, unfailing
pure and thrilling—
the meadow lark's call

recognized but
never the same
never quite caught
in the grasp
of ear
or mind
or heart
it sails across the fields
barely breaking
the surface
of consciousness

and so always, unfailing
the meadow lark's call

August

These mornings, something
burnished and sinewed
slides along the sun shafts
that glance between the drapes
pulled against the heat.

Wasps are working
the pendulous figs
amidst the high summer smells
of mowed lawns, hot asphalt,
and lightning.

These mornings, the fields
have begun to shrug and roll
with mist they've spent all night
conjuring from scant dew
and blessed cool.

These mornings reassure.
The turning, the slowing, the rotting,
the darkness will come again.

Into My Field

Pete the old bay horse
called to me this morning

not so that I could hear
but so that I could not look away

he stood apart from the others
as an old horse will

his ribs showed a bit
as an old horse's will

his russet face
with the white blaze

held so still–arrested while grazing
held my gaze without effort

and his black mane so lush
so thoroughly tossed

gave him a touch of wild
that wild that gathers these days

these fall days–translucent days
days of transubstantiation

> *all those things*
> *in your hands and your lap*
>
> *put them away*
> *come into my field*
>
> *and stay this time*
> *till you are cold and hungry*
>
> *and even then*
> *stay*

November Rain with Wind

Watch now!
The leaves
will fly off
The grass
will kneel down
and the colors
that take your breath
for sustenance—
watch! They are
going to ground
lumen by lumen.

Thanksgiving With My Son

Now in my
    old
    age
as limbs
    abandon expectation
    and long-held habit
as strength
    ignores imperative
    and will not uncoil
as mind
    steps sideways, retraces
    finds a different path
days become
    skewed, slanted
    seeking the gentlest incline

And to my astonishment
    here you are–
    graceful unbidden
placing your hand
    near mine as it
    searches for purchase
a steady warm body
    for me to tilt
    against
I never needed
    to ask
    nor explain
as though this were
foreordained
written in our genes
this turn-about
this counterpoise

Storm, Solstice

I

Sleet and wind take the farm
as night comes on
a misery of mud and shivering.
Pete the old bay horse
stands in the paddock
head lowered
coat darkened
tail pulled in.

Squinting into the sleet
I go to him
touch his shoulder to rouse him
slide a hand under his shaggy coat
feel his warmth there
tug his mane
walk him into the barn
into the steamy damp
and steady champing
of the other horses.
Rub him down
push him toward
the manger of hay.

As I head for the truck
I hear the patient clomp of hooves
as Pete heads back out into the storm.

II

Next morning
Pete stands at the crest of the hill
his wooly auburn coat set afire
by the low-riding Solstice sun
just clearing the horizon.
He has turned to look downslope
his breath wreaths
his wild black mane
his translucent ears.

And then crows
erupt yelling and cawing
from the creek bottom
splintering the frozen
hush over the field.
Pete arches his neck
dips his head
takes a few fancy steps
across the frozen slope.

Rough Beast, Christmas Eve

As I came up the farm road
night was shaking off the dusk
settling in the field. The owl
announced from the opaque
pines. The possum grunted
beneath the laden
persimmon tree.
An old field
an older moon
the persimmon's
lucent glow
the possum's
sparkling fur.

Horses on the Hillside

All four horses are down
hooves drawn up under chest and rump

muzzles resting on the cold earth
flanks offered to the watery sheen

of the early March sun which surprises
with the strength to finally push

each drowsy half-ton gelding
over on its side. They groan as they go over

heaving sighs and sweeping their cheeks
across the rough stubble.

They'll be well rested and ready tonight
when winter's last storm—gathering now

in the hills to the west—
roars down across the farm.

II. Long Covid

...stand as still as I can
with the light.

Still With the Light

First Sunday
after the first full moon
after the Spring Equinox
Easter morning for some
here on this particular land mass
so often a lovely day
at this latitude so often
a sort of gentleness
a willingness to smile
conveyed in the watery
green light that shimmers
and steps across
church lawns
and across my yard
where bluebirds jump
from the fence wire
into the broomsedge
and flutter back up
with crickets in their bills.

There is something else
shifting like clouds
below a horizon
insinuating just beyond
these Easter lawns—
something that would
come near now
if I let it
would bend this light
differently
would spurn
this morning's naive smile.

So I stand
as still as I can
with the light
the breeze shifting
the shadows
the bluebirds
dropping and rising
dropping and rising
that's all
just this holy light
just for now.

Retinue

Walking this wooded trail
with friends early that spring
keeping distance
but laughing and talking
each of us shepherding
our still-intact assumptions
along with us
like an invisible retinue—
our personas
our significance
surely who we were
      "... her peonies to the potluck... Pawleys Island in June... a
      beer every Friday... pick up the Times... season tickets..."

Today there is only
this old woman
her retinue scattered
fading off
into the woods.
There is this steep trail
gravel shifting
under foot
this gait weary
after weeks of illness
the light falling
through the canopy
dappling the slope
the cuckoos newly arrived
testing their clackity call
against the forest's echo
and the wind
at the crest of the hill
murmuring about the things
it gathers and spills
as it sweeps

from ridge to ridge.

Moment

I

I've put my mind
on a short leash today
not much I want
it poking into.
It doesn't seem to know
what's lurking out there
unanswerable
no safe harbor
so it would
wander too near
certain edges.

But if I keep my mind
here with just this
present moment—
email, the grocery order,
the weeds in the peony beds—
this day might pass
on an even keel.

II

There
is the meadow lark's aria—
so familiar yet
new every time—
sailing across the pasture.

There are the horses
bolting from the flies,
tossing their heads
and galloping into
the cool dark barn.

These bright
prayer flags
stirred by a breeze—
each flutter rippling peace
across the universe.

Dog Days

Trapped in the house
for the duration
this depleted
virus-ravaged body
will not tolerate
the heat of these
high summer days
I creep out only
before the sun clears
the eastern tree line
or after it is long gone
from the evening sky

But then
one morning in August
I will glimpse
that inchoate slant
to the light
smell that nuance
of ripe figs
and of green
gone past its prime
and that night
I'll hear the coyotes
at the pond
and although the heat
will persist and the dust
will not settle
everything
oh everything
will have changed

It's Lughnasa

All shall be well, and all shall be well,
and all manner of thing shall be well.
                                        —*Julian of Norwich*

and there are the geese
testing the rhythm
of their call and response
that will lift them
by the score in unison
one day in October.

And there is the light
shifting the field's palette
from bright to golden
its slant lifting
deeper shades
to the surface
to touch and spring from
bluestem and goldenrod.

Out in the field
goldfinches flock
and disperse, flock again
their season's work

finally done.
A cohort of new-fledged
indigo buntings flashes
up from the broomsedge
sparring—a flurry
of wings and claws
like joy rising and falling.

And yes, there will be
days of pressing heat
the Rudbeckia will wilt
and fade and gasp and persist
the figs will ripen for the coyotes
or rot as the wasps move in.

The bay horse circles
the birch in the pasture
leans his graceful bulk
against the trunk
and rubs at summer's
residue of dust and irritation

but I know on this
Lughnasa morning
that I will be well
that all will be well
that all of these things
will be well.

Weather

This cold—
its weight is too much.
Carried by waves of rain
descending like harpies
from scudding dark places
into this morning
that will not dawn.

What part
of this morning
is just the weather
what part is fear
of the dark and the cold
of sliding away
of coming undone.

It's just weather
just winter.

Winter Soltice I

Before first light
before the mocking
bird's call rends
this foggy stillness,

my footsteps
along the gravel path
lend heft to the silence.

Through a breach
in the fog I see
Venus deepening
the darkness.

Not knowing what else
could follow night, I wait
once more for dawn.

Blood Work

So they've drawn blood again
several vials this time.
Back out in the parking lot
January's knife—
a whipping northerly wind—
lends brilliant clarity
to the corporeal:
the prickle of wool at the chin
the throb of winter-cracked fingers
finding keys in silky
pocket lining
the insistence
of a cantering heart
the thick gauze pad taped
inside my elbow.

Those vials of blood
lined up in their rack
produced in these bones
and cells by
some wizardry
some alchemy
these bones
are cold and stiff now
as they move
into the wind
towards the car

Tell them, please
in your cryptic lab-speak
cRP, CK, dsDNA—please
can you tell them this time
what it is.

A hospital parking lot
one place a person
weeping in their car
would be no cause for alarm
plenty of reasons
most better than this.

Great Horned Owl

The sun's not up yet
and it's sleeting.
I let the old slow dog
out into it.
Here in the kitchen
there's cold and dark enough
to fill my heart and more.
Tik tik tikking
at the blank windows.

I open the door
to let the dog back in
she shakes—a halo
of icey droplets—
and I hear the deep
hoo hooing
of the great horned owl
soft, mutable, unassuming
what I've been listening for
all winter.

Sleet

Hunkered low and deep
a heron at the edge
of the pond
the hard rain
turning to sleet
she holds her ground

> *Many years ago*
> *a winter morning*
> *of brittle brightness*
> *ice holding*
> *the creek in thrall*
> *frozen pine limbs*
> *cracking high above*
> *I came upon a heron's*
> *body undisturbed*
> *crouched it seemed*
> *in a tangle of roots*
> *below the creek bank*
> *I took it home*
> *those hollow bones*
> *that fierce yellow beak*
> *those taffeta feathers*
> *dusky blue gray and*
> *unexpected peach*
> *both of us so young*

Now the sleet accrues
coating the willow twigs
but she holds her ground
holding me rapt
Oh to slip inside
the stillness
of that hunched silhouette

A Healing

Sometimes I think
there's an old woman
in the woods
I (might) have seen her.

(She or) someone
once left
a heap of black walnuts
at the foot of my garden
and when
I approached
crows (it seemed)
flapped away
flashing indigo
into the woods

or was it (her)
someone's robe
and (maybe)
a cloth sack
hanging black
from (her) shoulder.

I dreamed of that sack
I drew it with charcoal
brushed it grey
with wash as I'd seen

my mother do with
her watercolors.
So early one morning
I waited at the edge
of the woods
it had snowed in the night
and soon it would rain
and fog was falling
through the dripping trees.
Crows erupted
from shaggy branches
cawing alarm or
(maybe) laughing (at me).

When (she) opened (her) bag
proffered its emptiness
I unwound
my illness
from around
my shoulders
and let it
fall in.

The crows
strutted and postured
in the melting snow
and at some signal
all rose and dispersed
into the sifting fog.

In Late February

there is always
a wind in the woods
a basso continuo hum,

the fugue the chorus frogs
play toccata against,
the sound memory makes

when it wakes and rises
up through the earth
towards sleeping roots.

The field has forgotten
about summer and bees
and lightning.

But the trees,
whose roots are deepest,
are remembering something

and the frogs,
whose sleep is the lightest,
are dying to hear it.

Of course February
would sing like this
whether I heard it or not.

But again this year
I am here in the field,
at the edge of the woods.

Threshold

Winter takes an excursion
into spring—brief, flashy
accompanied by chorus
frogs and woodcocks
in the wet fields
bluebirds iridescing
on the fence wire—

then returns
in a day or so
with a scattering
of scant flakes that
upon touching down
disappear into
sogginess.

As the wind
swings back around
to northerly
something sighs
(my age perhaps)
at this reprieve
spared—at least for now—
from the irrepressible
burgeoning.

Hyacinths in the Grass

These points of lapis
scattered through the new
spring grass—certainly
they are beautiful.
Certainly the mauve haze
of the winged elm
ringing the meadow
is also beautiful. And
the fuchsia smears
of the redbud trees
against the lingering silence
of the winter woods—
all so beautiful.
But spring no longer thrills me.

It is good
to see confirmed
the integrity, the resilience
of this turning once again.
It reassures, it pleases, delights.
But it no longer thrills me.

The stir and rush
of inchoate promise
seems to have shifted—
traversed the seasons
from chirruping green
through a bright and brutal apex
and come to rest instead
amidst the falling down
the gentle rotting
the potent promise
of endings.

Vaccinated

An old woman
long-uncut hair
falling across papery
pale face
inches her way
out of her car
in the co-op parking lot
kids whiz by on bikes
music beats
from an open window
someone calls to a friend—
a masked hug, laughter, delight.

The old woman
peers over her N-95
squints in the sunlight
holding to the door frame
takes tentative steps
away from the car
jeans hang off her hips
she clutches her grocery bags
checks her list
follows two young women
in yoga clothes
into the humming store.

After the Year We've Had

Well there's no getting around it
once again it's early May

with those puffy clouds and the wind
spring wind—wind like no other

whooshing across the meadow
stirring the new grass into undulations

flattening it down along the slough
like a river current

taking the bend at the fence
with swirls of silky froth

while the pines make pinesong
exhalations of aaaahhh and haaahhh

rising, celebratory, receding
to sing among themselves

then emerging again with whispered roar
no there's no denying it, the stuff of spring—

that unabashed going out into the meadow
tumbling along with the grassy current

and tipping up to the circling hawks
raising my arms, leaning, kettling

can this be, after the year we've had
(are still having)

here is May and the wind
and the grass and the hawks

and I'm in this current
can this be happiness, even so

How Far to Look

The storm approaches
from the southeast
fleeing its own disaster

I venture out onto the porch
to take a look at the wind and rain
mounting against an iron sky

On the deck
the chairs are pulled back
against the wall

Quickening prayer flags
are releasing peace
across the back meadow

And the rain–oh the blessed rain–
falls steadily on withered fields
and desolated woods

Good fortune wherever I look
as long as I look
only as far as my eye can see

Say what you will

but when I walked out
to the mailbox
to see if this
blighted old body
would make it
that far and back again,
as I reached
the top of the rise
where the birch-lined lane
rounded the bend
left the shade
and burst
into the glaring field
into the tyrant blaze
of the first spring day
that harbingered summer,
I felt a breeze
gather behind me
then sweep me along
fully bodily carrying me
weary limping dizzy
down the last stretch home.
And it felt like more than just
a stroke of luck.

Still Might Be

As though you've been away for a long time—
some sort of internment or seclusion—
you've lost that readiness with words
with topics of conversation
lost that facility with a smile
lift of brow or tilt of chin
your mind grown accustomed
to the simple imperative of
one step at a time
okay or not okay

But here at this little table on this café patio
these are your old friends and their eyes
clear and steady, hold yours
as they ask and nod, touch your wrist
there on the table next to your mug of tea
you lift the mug, set it down amidst
their words and laughter
they are reminding you
who you were
still might be.

III. Each to Each

...out of this field,
out of this body, this mind, this heart...

After reading the news I am here in this unmown meadow

feeling the muck take hold of my step
smelling the dogfennel's bitter medicine
hearing the sparrow's protesting tut-tut
as I brush past its nest.

I find no moral high ground here
just an infinity of getting and making
of taking and tearing
and letting go.

In the grass in the slough in the stand of pines
life and death are finally accountable
part of a bargain–a consummate bargain
made each to each.

I Am Grass Lying Down

A doe steps along
through the grass
stopping here or here
tugging at stems, lipping blades.

The fawn follows her.
New pink lips, tiny teeth
clasp and nip. A trail follows them
through the grass.

Coyote comes trotting
nose to ground, shoulders flared
following the trail
through the grass.

I am grass lying down
angle-bent to the baked ground
green sublimes, suppleness wanes
like a tide going out.

If You're Lucky, Your Heart Will Break

—Jack Kornfield

Humming birds hover
      in the buckeye blooms.
A pair of otters
      has made its silvery scent mound
      at the edge of the pond.
And the familiar lone heron
      arrived today with two others along—
      flapping for purchase in the trees,
      parachuting into the shallows.
There is no message of doom here.
      Natural disasters are
      just items in the news.

We're careful here to keep
the water clean, the food chain intact.
Our stream is buffered.
We use no pesticides.
We don't kill snakes.
Don't mow the fields
until the nestlings have fledged.

To step back
from this pond
these fields
this farm—
to shed this smaller sense of home
to see that it has not been enough
this breaks my heart.

Witness

Deep in the woods
on the steepest slope
shining beech
overcup oak
shagbark hickory
day after day
the rending mayhem
of screaming machines
the singing of treetops
falling through hot summer air
the tremendous booming
as one after the other
they thunder to earth.

> *If you press your ear*
> *against a tree*
> *in summer*
> *you can hear*
> *its watery life*
> *coursing*
> *through the phloem.*
> *In winter*
> *there is silence.*

At the edge of the clear-cut
around the perimeter
huge old oaks and hickories
are rooted in witness
they are leaning in
opening their giant limbs
to the unprecedented
light and air

Leave It at That

Cuckoo's call
my favorite of all
for its demure
powk-powk
as though
the deep shade itself
was uttering
something of a song.

And then its bright
and worldly
clackity-clack
(no song at all)
seems it could
emanate as well
from the wicked yellow bill
as from the soft gray throat.

No longer any need
to pronounce its name
or to call to mind
the checkered pattern
of the long and elegant tail.

Just to hear—
and leave it at that
a passing moment's
play upon the air
upon the wooded dapples.

Here Is What's Left

Summer wanes as usual
the Rudbeckia succumbs
to mildew and wilt
the figs fall
under the weight
of sucking junebugs
the pond is muddy
scummed over and still
even the birds are quiet
their calls diminished

Looking out
at the brittle grass
in the crickety field
I see scraps and tatters
of old assumptions
of unearned grace
being dragged away
with the season's remnants:
a semblance of security here
a shadow of normalcy there
pieces of convenience
disjointed shapes
of good times
all crumbling
as they go
leaving a light breeze
to stir the stillness

amidst the nodding
muhly grass plumes

So then
here is what's left
the grass
the breeze
the slipping light
the emptiness
whose touch is so gentle
the kindness of it all

Apprentice

After David Whyte

Even now at Summer Solstice
the transparency of the morning
is apparent.

Color slides from shape to shape
and shapes elide the fixing attention
of the eye

just as they would on an unmoored
autumn morning of drift and fog
and senescence

or in the slip and flash of shadow
across winter's hard brilliance.
In such light

it seems *I might become
an apprentice to the arc of my own
disappearance.*

It's not autumn yet

but still the light
inclining across the lawn
has something added
or maybe something taken
away. It (the light)
alludes to something

Cicadas and phoebes say their names   cuckoos clack
from deep in the woods   fox musk thickens the sulky air
wasps drill and suck the vulvic figs

that can be taken or let go.
I stand still now,
careful not to make
a meaning of it (this light),
and it opens up the crown
of my head with a sound
like wind in pines.

Goldenrod Light

This
is not just the weather
this goldenrod light
this juniper breeze
this cadence of
crow-speak
at the edge
of the woods

Nor is it just the season
this perfection
of air against brow
of a hawk's red tail
against lapis sky
mere season
cannot account
for this opening in time
this unfolding of mind

I feel the meadow sway
stem against stem
I watch from
the gibbous moon's
day-pale advantage
the coming together
the turning
the parting

Running

I held the undisputed title
of the fastest kid
in second grade
but one fall morning
as I sped down our
makeshift kickball field
of unmown grass tangled with
unraked sycamore leaves
Annie Scott with blond curls
and green eyes appeared
at my side overtaking me
I heard her breath
felt her palpable presence
distinct corporeal
her stride matched mine
we both grinned laughed
ran on through the leaves
forgetting the ball
each stretching racing flying
it was I believe
my first taste of ecstasy

Decades later
it seems I ran
only in my dreams
with lead weights on my legs
through waist-deep molasses
or wet cement
one summer at the beach
sharks appeared in the surf
their wicked black fins
so horrible my granddaughter
out there oblivious on her float
I strained and churned
against the waves
to reach her
my body leaden
my mind gone wild
those dreams coming true

Now I am old
I can no longer run
but my dreams
these days
are light and strong
can be carried along
into waking
and in my dreams
I fly again sometimes
my feet lose touch
with the ground
I rise above
the sycamore trees
and there below
is the field of grass
and the leaves
and the children running

Again, This Time of Year

walking toward that place
in the woods–yours–
because it's October

the colors are gathering
slipping through the woods
and you among them–the colors–

here you are again
because it's October
come to hone my memories

to burnish them–my memories–
neither of us looks
at me or at my life but only

at the moving light in the trees
and the colors sliding
slipping through the woods

each year these glimpses of you
are more clear more bright
they linger longer–these glimpses–

and the going back out of the woods
seems of less account–the going back–
it weighs less each time

and these clefts that are opening
lead out and up–these openings
among the slipping colors

and still I miss you–wait
why do I say 'still'–as though
it will ever end–the missing

Winter Solstice II

Heron croaks, flies up from her roost.
A star unmoors, sails east.
No sign yet of dawn.
Gray foxes whoop and whoop
loping, looping through
the frost-thralled fields.
If I let darkness
hold me still and close,
it empties me of waiting.

All the Winter Mornings

Dawn comes searching
across the fields
touching the sky
the clouds the darkness–
like blind fingers
shaping out the day–
the tree tops
the frosted tangles
of sumac and briar
the crouching cedars.

The great horned owl
holds steady witness
Hoo and-a-hoo, Hoo Hoo
her cadence
filling me with lightness.

How to tell her
she is heard
how to keep her
safe and close
in this paltry patch
of woods
calling up
Christmas morning
calling up
all the winter mornings.

Into Winter Sun

Sitting still at the south window
and meadow larks rise exulting
out of the winter-silver field as if
newly created they are born
and rise into the blinding
winter sun that wheels low
across the southern sky
and everything

everything rises with the larks
out of this field and out of this body
this mind, this heart
they too–body mind heart—
rise and are gone with the larks
into the blind white morning

Waning Gibbous Moon

Well past Winter Solstice
waning gibbous moon
and an ice storm coming on.
A few little dickie birds
fuss at the feeder
but nothing stirs in the meadow
no peepers in the slough, not even
the zeep of mating woodcocks—
still a few weeks off.

It seems this time of year
has nothing much to say
the woods are finally
looking shabby
their nakedness worn thin
just the frigid dead of winter
a string of unsung days
safekeeping spring.

East Window

An instant—sunrise—
those first few seconds
when light flashes
straight and true across
the frost-thralled field
one single blade
one crystal of ice
splintered
clearing away
sleep, yes, but also
the familiar mind—
industrious, judicious, precious
bounded by what it knows.
That instant, that light,
that clearing.

Shaking Off the Pall

> *That the self advances*
> *And confirms ten thousand things*
> *Is called delusion;*
> *That the ten thousand things*
> *Advance and confirm the self*
> *Is called enlightenment.*
>
> *—Dogen*

Frost this morning
could pass for snow
if only the light
is considered
They say this light–
just as the sun
mounts the horizon
to swing along
its low winter arc–
this light is the brightest.

The best
for shaking off
the pall of winter
its weight
its turned-away shoulder
its indifference
to my need for warmth
for something next

But sometimes
the winter field
is just grass–
bleached and dry
the wind in the grass
is just that–
heedless and chill
the birds are the same–
familiar and plain.

Turn again and turn again
the killdeers cry out
and circle the field
the wind runs in
quickens the grass
their stems shiver and glint
their leaves twitch and spring
the watcher just one
of these ten thousand things

Like Wind Into Air

The wind and the lark
a stillness inside the wind
silence in the song

not simply respite
but something wider
than this field–a going in

like the meadow lark
into the wind I would go
like wind into air

Acknowledgments

I gratefully acknowledge the generous critique and guidance of the Poet Fools and the Lorax Poets; the indispensable critical eye of Roxanne Henderson; and, above all, the unflagging belief of Gail Straub and David Gershon.

About the Author

Joanie McLean is an ecologist and poet who lives in Silk Hope, North Carolina. She holds degrees in Botany from UNC - Chapel Hill and in Wetland Ecology from Duke University. She is the winner of the New Millennium Writings Prize for Poetry, and a three time finalist for the James Applewhite Poetry Prize. Her poems have appeared in and won awards from many journals and magazines. *Like Wind Into Air* is her 4th poetry collection and winner of an Honorable Mention for the NC Poetry Society's Lena Shull Book Award. (www.joaniemclean. com)

www.ingramcontent.com/pod-product-compliance
Lightning Source LLC
Chambersburg PA
CBHW031148090426
42738CB00008B/1264